MW01242783

Philosophies of Daily Living

Mark A. Schrader

Thanks to Mom and Dad and Big Brother and Wife Lady and the Little Schraders. Without all of you I would not be who I am.

Introduction to Philosophies of Daily Living

Within these pages, you'll find a collection of essays ranging from self-awareness to parenting and some contemplation on values and time.

I'm unsure if I can pinpoint a genre to assign this writing other than my identification in the title "Philosophies of Daily Living."

In my advice and financial planning industry, I often come across the term "Activities of Daily Living" or ADLs. ADLs are the main human activities people need to take care of themselves. These terms are generally used in healthcare to refer to how people can provide self-care.

Depending on your source, you can find different numbers out there that constitute how many ADLs there are, but the basic list includes:

Bathing

Dressing

Toileting

Transferring (getting in and out of bed or chair)

Eating

Continence

I've come across these in my insurance training and studies, as those are also measures that insurance companies use to determine eligibility for some benefits.

I had a feeling a few years back that I needed to write down my language for what was beyond the Activities of Daily Living.

I wanted to describe self-awareness in the way ADLs describe self-care. I noticed there wasn't enough self-awareness going around.

I can't say I had a specific goal or title at the start, but that's just it. I had to start. You have to start the things you want to finish.

I hope you find value in reading these essays on the Philosophies of Daily Living. Each essay's goal is to make you think about questions that are important to you. I haven't tried to radiate you with any tactics to implement because I don't know your personality or circumstances. I've tried to frame concepts broadly in my way, which hopefully will inspire you to think in your own way.

I don't expect that each essay will have an immediate impact, though I hope you'll give each a read and filter what questions make you think.

We're all in different parts of our journeys.

I'd like this to be as much an experience and an opportunity to reflect as it is something to read. For that purpose, I've left one blank page after each essay for you to write your reactions. I didn't even put lines there because I want you to write in any direction you choose.

This also is a short book.

I know some will question the length of a published work, but my goal was not to satisfy a word count. It was to make this project approachable and something that could travel with you, the reader, as you go through your journey—hopefully resonating with different questions at different times.

Why Philosophies of Daily Living?

The tenets of Solid

Mainstreaming PDLs: Expanding the boundaries of what we think of when making choices. Opening the world to a broader audience and relating self-awareness to everyday decisions and personal values. Making conversations more approachable.

The realism standard of the PDLs

So much "advice" and so many conversations we are fed or that we have are not realistic. Absolutes and ultimatums are good for bumper stickers but not good for Life and decision making. Do not fall prey to bumper sticker judgment and bumper sticker planning.

Positive messages of Life. Aligning decision making with personal values. Instead of taking negative misdirection from the loudest voices, seek to finding positive reasons to make decisions vs negative reasons not to make decisions.

The Nature of PDLs

It's every day. It's ongoing. Where you are now may not be inside your control but where to go and how you plan from right now is going to be an accumulation of choices that are still in front of you.

(life and decision making) are like time travel.

If you're ever read or seen any discussion about time travel, you've heard of the butterfly effect. The butterfly effect basically states that the fluttering of a butterfly's wing in the past can grow and change the wind elsewhere. Basically (from google), the phenomenon whereby a minute, local change in a complex system can have large effects elsewhere. Activities you take today ripple forward into the future and may have unexpected outcomes. Certainly, we try to forecast those effects with what we know about the past and present but future outcomes may be altered by unknowns we cannot see. Preparation for future outcomes are influenced by decisions you make now.

Because when you are floating in the ocean, taking your last gasps, you don't look into the sky for a rocket ship to grab onto. You reach for something solid. When you reach something solid you can look up.

(it's easier to plan the path up the mountain when you are in base camp and not hanging from the ledge).

Because life often feels like a mudslide. Slipping slowly away. Sometime quicker than others. The landscape shifts around you. Features of your surroundings get covered by the mudslide, new things are revealed and your perspective changes as it all shifts around you.

Embrace the Journey

Write things down.

Contemporaneous Notes
Do you remember everything?

I'm thinking a lot today about a way to keep your head when it's stormy and things are flying all around you.

(Write things down)

You get to where you are today by the decisions you've made

Good and Bad.

Do you remember what you were thinking at these decision points?

Did you take notes?

Remembering the why of a particular decision or choice can help you evaluate its current progress or outcome.

A quick internet search gives this definition of contemporaneous notes:

Contemporaneous notes are notes made at the time or shortly after an event occurs. They represent the best recollection of what you witnessed

I would add that it also helps you remember what you

were feeling at the time.

Contemporaneous Notes help to understand your experience and thought process at a specific point in time.

Do you remember everything?

I've heard from various sources in my life that "if it's not written down it didn't happen."

One small example here could be all the stuff laying around your house.

What discussions led to getting all that stuff you have?

What did you list as your goals at that time for acquiring that stuff?

Were those things for temporary enjoyment? Were those things for family heirlooms?

I'm not as concerned about what your actual things are but why you chose them and whether they still meet the goals. Your goals.

Have these goals changed?

So how do you keep notes?

Maybe you have a notes app?

Keep a notebook?

Maybe a journal or a diary?

Have you ever tried journaling your daily feelings/events so you can remember? I try sometimes but don't always manage to keep it up daily.

It's a shared human trait that we don't always remember why we drove decisions that led to bad outcomes. We may not realize we need to change our process.

We do remember if we drove decisions that led to a good outcome...but do we remember how we made those choices? Or are we just that good?

So we get to where we are today by the decisions we've made.

Good and Bad.

Do we remember what we were thinking at these decision points?

Did we take notes?

If we want to remember the "why" of a decision and remember what we were feeling at the time.

(Write things down)

Make Contemporaneous notes

Acknowledge the Truth

It Broke
A quick reflection on self and parenting

When I was young, I was famous (or infamous) in my house for a specific phrase I would use when explaining something to my parents.

"It Broke."

Now I can't remember any specific item this happened with or any cute anecdote or story. I think it was a kid's way of not accepting fault for his own (or my own) actions.

Dad would ask me what happened, and I would say, "It Broke."

Now, of course, my Dad would straighten me out and remind me that generally, things don't just break.

"It Broke" was not an acceptable answer for my Mom and Dad.

I needed to acknowledge not that "It Broke" but that "I Broke It."

My actions led to the item breaking in most cases, and my parents wanted me to acknowledge the truth of the matter and be accountable for my own actions.

Next time you think something has happened to you, think through the situation, and ask yourself:

Did It Break? Or did my action lead to it breaking?

PHILOSOPHIES OF DAILY LIVING

We all need a professor in our lives

Find Your Professor

A thank you to a coworker

I like to think I'm knowledgeable about the topics that I study.

I like to think I have an expert's ability to read the information on my topics and process it at a very high level. I might even find areas where I would consider myself an expert from time to time.

I know the fundamentals of my work.

I can usually diagnose issues or find ways to course-correct if something appears off track.

I know what is important.

What I also know is that:

I'm not always the smartest person in the room.

Some people read a bit more than I do. Some people don't stream as much as I do. Some people don't watch sports as much as I do (Keep Pounding). There are people like this in your profession as well who have deep knowledge and take extra care in understanding their profession.

I have a coworker that I will call here:

"The Professor."

I'm talking about the colleague that not only has the books on their desk but has also dog-eared multiple pages in each book.

You know who I'm talking about.

Picture this person in your mind. They are an expert resource whenever something is gnawing at the edge of your brain. Whenever you think you are on the right track and just need a nice nod of validation to keep you on your way.

You need this person. I need this person. We all need a professor in our lives.

I don't mean someone to lecture you on a topic. I don't mean someone to instruct you which direction to go. I'm talking about the person who has done the work, who has done the reading, and who can help you analyze the problem that is staring you in the face.

Can you picture this person in your office?

You may recognize them by phrases such as:
1. "have you thought about it like this?"

2. "Let's take another look."
3. "What is the question we're trying to answer?"

This is the person who can help you reset your perspective when you are staring down a question so hard that you lose the outline of the shape of the question and have trouble remembering why you are asking the question.

Take a deep breath, sit back for a moment and reach out to the Professor. "Hey Professor, can I get your opinion on something?"

Look around at work and see who you can find.

Everyone should find their professor.

You'll be glad you did.

Seek better content

Are you an authority?

Finding your voice

I've been thinking recently of the way content providers/writers communicate with their readers.

When you as a reader are looking for answers to your questions, what type of provider are you hoping to find?

1. Do they speak with Authority?

Or

2. Do they speak with Authority?

I know it appears I've asked the same question twice, but from the dictionary I pulled a couple of definitions of the word "Authority."

The first definition I came across is:

Authority:

"the power or right to give orders, make decisions, and enforce Obedience."

This definition has synonyms of power, jurisdiction, command, control, charge, dominance, rule, sovereignty, supremacy.

WOW.

That isn't the way I want my providers to speak to me. Supremacy? Power? Dominance? If that is the relationship you have it's probably time to reconsider.

The third definition (the second is also good but doesn't factor into today's discussion) is:

Authority:

"the power to influence others, especially because of one's commanding manner or one's recognized knowledge about something."

This is the type of authority I want to read. Based on "one's recognized knowledge about something."

Confidence. Knowledge. An expert in the subject.

When you are looking for answers to your questions, what type of provider are you hoping to find?

I know I'm parsing words, but I wanted to explore this idea in writing.

Thinking about asking questions and how those questions are answered is one of my goals.

When you're seeking answers to your questions, what

voice are you hoping to hear?

Do they answer in a manner of someone who has power or supremacy over you and assumes superiority?

Or do they answer as someone who is a knowledgeable expert on the subject?

I think this is an important distinction. When you are seeking content, I would expect the provider to partner with you in your success.

I want them to be an authority on the subject and not an authority who views you as the subject to be ruled who is lucky to be talking to them and assume all control in the situation.

As a reader this question has driven me to seek better content.

How about you?

This leads to a final ask of those of us who are readers and also writers.

When you create content:

1. Do you speak with Authority?

Or

2. Do you speak with Authority?

Make yourself some space

Give Yourself Air

Life needs oxygen

Give yourself space to make choices.

Give yourself air.

How many times when we are facing a choice do we tighten up? We hunker down and think so hard about an option, and the decision gets harder.

We concentrate.

We push ourselves.

We get tunnel vision on this one decision that we want to make.

We lose perspective.

We focus so hard on a specific idea or task or choice that sometimes we lose our overriding goal.

I propose that you must give yourself air.

The decisive fire inside you shouldn't be cramped. It shouldn't be in such a small place that it starts to flicker out.

I've felt this way recently.

My creative fires have been smoldering.

I'm less decisive. Less innovative than I used to be.

I need some space.

I need air.

There is a reason the Emma Lazarus poem is so powerful:

"give me your tired, your poor, your huddled masses."

And this is the point I'm talking about today,

"Yearning to breathe free."

Yes, there is much more to that poem, but I'm just focusing on that yearn we all have. That affects our day to day life. That alters our day to day decision making. "Yearning to breathe free."

Not yearning to "be" free. Yearning to "breathe" free.

All of us have a feeling in our ordinary day to day life where choices and decisions feel made for us without our input — guided by unseen hands.

Now you may think I'm overly dramatic. But many of our

choices in this modern environment feel that way.

Just a few options. None good. Lesser of two evils kind of decisions.

I suggest here today that we all step away and back off the tunnel vision.

Knock a sunroof in your smoldering cave of indecision.

Get some perspective.

Make yourself some space. I know we all yearn to breathe free.

Give yourself air.

Maybe it's a vacation.

Maybe just a long weekend. Perhaps a night off work or a night out on the town when you wouldn't usually go out.

Maybe it's a walk in the woods or a hike in the mountains.

Take some time for yourself. Open up that perspective. Step away and pause a moment on that decision you've been trying to make. Gain some additional perspective.

Maybe you don't have to make this decision alone?

Give Yourself Air.

...

One more way to think about it:

Do you ever get a coffee or drink with a solid lid and a little space to drink from, and you go for the first sip and get a tiny drop?

A barely satisfying little drop pops out? Have you ever had that happen?

I know someone out there understands.

The cafeteria at work where I get my morning coffee changed out their lids a few months back, and I noticed each morning I wasn't getting a healthy sip.

I found this very frustrating. So I did my thing. I paused. I evaluated. And it took me a few minutes to understand what was happening. When they switched the lids out with the new batch, the air holes in the top were smaller. Maybe a manufacturing issue. Perhaps a design issue. But without the correct air, the liquid would not flow. I did what any Solid person would do, and I took my keys out and made the air hole larger.

I gave myself air.

I think it works similarly in decision making:

You pause.

You evaluate.

You take time to understand.

Do your thing.

It's like a fire that has plenty of wood and fuel. You still need to stoke it and blow air on the coals.

Give Yourself Air.

Everyone has a different personality and preferences

Understanding You do You

What does it mean to you?

I've heard this phrase lately, and I wanted to explore what it means.

I didn't think much of it the first time I heard it, and I don't even remember the context. It seemed innocuous enough that it didn't really impact me much one way or another.

It seemed positive to me.

You Do You

You do what makes you happy.

You Do You.

Everyone has a different personality and preferences.

You interact with the world through your lens. You do the things that match up with your thoughts, goals, and vision for your place in the world.

Sounds pretty cool to me.

What a simple phrase! It almost entirely explains the view that we are all individuals in this world with fully realized thoughts and feelings and hopes and dreams.

This phrase is out there to reassure us that there is support for our endeavors through a common mantra.

Positive Mental Attitude!

You Do You!

But alas, I find more and more that my internal take on things might be overwhelmingly positive where positive may not win the day.

Positive is me doing me.

Positive is my general setting for interpreting the world. Still, as I get older, I learn that isn't always the case for everyone else.

I was talking about this phrase with my wife recently. I thought "You Do You" was a beautiful thing like "Go for it" or "You got this" or "YOLO" (you only live once)- which may need its own conversation at another time, but I don't want to digress too much now.

I used the phrase "You Do You," and my wife bristled a bit. She didn't feel I had used it correctly. She thought I had inserted it incorrectly into the conversation.

She felt I had taken a generally positive conversation and added in the negative phrase "You Do You" right in the middle.

Without going into further detail of what was said, she questioned me on the usage of the term.

I explained my generally positive understanding, and she, as she tends to do, gave me a broader perspective on the world.

You see, my wife and I are both generally positive and on the same page. At moments like these, we work well because we have complementary skill sets along with different views and perspectives.

She had heard the phrase "You Do You" in other contexts. From her perspective, from the settings she had heard it used, it was pejorative. It was expressing contempt or disapproval. It was disparaging and derogatory.

I'll say I was a bit shocked. I have these moments from time to time when I hear new takes on ideas, I thought I understood. I learned once again that my perspective could always grow just a little broader.

I don't tell this story to bring up how wonderful my wife is (which she is) but to open the conversation more around different perspectives.

Perspectives

Do you view things through a positive lens?

Do you view things through a negative lens?

Does your lens need cleaning?

You Do You.

Time passes differently on vacation.

Giant Dishwasher for the Brain

Where do you find it?

I want to share the week I'm having with everyone who is reading this.

I'd like you to know and understand how I'm feeling right now. I'm on day 3 of a full week-long beach vacation, and I feel great. Now when I say I'd like to share it, I don't mean I want to invite more people here. No offense intended, but since it's a vacation with the in-laws, there are already enough people in the house. Mostly, people I like.

What I mean is I would like to share the feeling. I want everyone to know this feeling. I want everyone to understand how the days slow down (although the week goes by at hyper speed). I want everyone to feel the reordering of priorities. I want everyone to be able to know the temporal disruption.

The waves at first seem a bit loud and too constant. The wind seems maybe a bit strong and overly active. But at some point, as you watch the waves...at some point, as the sand pounds your senses...at some point, as the wind continues to blow your skin...at some point, it's just right. Just sitting by the ocean for me is one of the most calming, clarifying endeavors I can undertake in this modern world.

Don't get me wrong. I know it's not for everyone. I know other people find their beach elsewhere. And I don't want to overstate the simplicity of sitting on the beach. I know there can be dangers lurking offshore. I know there are dangers in extreme sun exposure. I know there are in-laws literally standing in the middle of the kitchen, in hallways, blocking stairwells, and filling up the public spaces.

Or is that just me?

I'm digressing a bit with the in-laws, but I don't want to get too off track. This is a great trip that we take each year. Time with family visiting a beach town we come to every summer. It's a circuit breaker from the ordinary course of everyday lives.

Just like anywhere else, there is a routine here

- Breakfast with family
- Time on the beach
- Come in for lunch
- Some days a side trip or more time on the beach
- Showers
- Out for dinner
- Maybe some games then conversation once the kids

go to bed

Seems so simple. How can that be a transformational feeling that I wish I could share with everyone?

And no, I don't need a ton of messages reminding me I didn't mention sunscreen. Part of the time in the beach routine is the slathering on or spraying (thank goodness for spray sunscreen) of the SPF 30 or more to make sure no one gets overly tender. My wife is the leader in the sunscreen brigade. She oversees putting the stuff on the kid's faces, and sometimes arms and I come along with the spray to finish things off.

The feeling I'm talking about isn't just the temporal disruption. Though I know some scientist somewhere would probably argue that the minutes and hours are the same, time passes differently on vacation at the beach.

Drive to the beach, go to bed. Wake up, drive home. But somehow a whole week has gone by in what feels like one night.

Back to that feeling. I want to share but can't seem to describe it. The ocean, the waves, the wind. It's like a cleaner somehow. Like you get all the residue of daily work life, everyday school life, daily tasks, regular day to day, everything in your typical environment. This stuff builds up! It cakes in your brain like residue on a pot that you've used for supper this evening.

It isn't horrible stuff. It doesn't hurt you, but it starts to build up. The beach vacation, for me, is a giant dishwasher for my brain. Place yourself in the right wind, the right water, the right spray, and you run multiple cycles.

The first day, the everyday tasks loosen up a bit in your mind. The next day a little bit less is holding on. Repeat the cycle, and all of a sudden that task list at home or the cubicle you sit in or those emails waiting on the work computer…they fall away.

I guess that may be a bit of a leap for some. But for me, that's how a vacation at the beach works.
For you maybe it's camping, or hiking, or a cabin in the mountains. Perhaps it's a cruise ship or a tropical island.

For me it is the beach.

Where is your giant dishwasher for the brain?

It isn't about you

The Building of Sandcastles and The Digging of Holes

A personal reflection on self and parenting

As a Dad on the beach, there are certain expectations.

Expectations differ depending on your family situation. My wife and I are both heavily involved with the kids. It's a great honor to fulfill my obligations. The word *"obligations"* here is in no way intended to be negative. I use it to describe what I do as Dad.

One obligation with young children is to keep the kids actively engaged while Mom is resting.

I pictured myself as the type of super-engaged Dad that would impress his children and the passerby with prowess in sandcastle building. I would design a structure in which my children's imagination could grow and flourish while cultivating exceptional and exquisite fantasy worlds to explore. I considered myself to be above average in creativity, and I never worried about the skill set. My handiness would help me build and develop as the kids got older.

I knew this was something I could do.

I knew this was something I would do and that I would do it well.

I couldn't wait to build magical memories for my kids to tell their kids about (and possibly even their grandkids). I could already envision it and hear their tales:

"You should have seen what our Dad used to build for us. They were huge! The greatest and most impressive sandcastles on the beach."

Perhaps I overthink things from time to time. I was impressed with these sandcastles before I built them.

The excitement was palpable the first time we walked on the beach when the boy was old enough to play in the sand. I was going to be amazing. I bought the proper sand toys with castle formations. When filled and turned over multiple times in the appropriate order, I knew they would rival anything occupied by Queen Elizabeth II. Though I don't have any specific memories from when I was that age, this was going to be memorable for the boy.

I started digging the dirt to fill the molds. I raised the first wall of the castle structure. I stood back to take in the cornerstone of my sandcastle building destiny.

Then I saw the glee on the boy's face as he stomped his foot directly through the center of my accomplishment.

I was dismayed.

I thought, "I'll *teach him how to build, and we'll build together.*"

After a quick admonishment, I explained that we needed to leave these walls alone so we could build our castle. I proceeded to make the next line of the castle.

Then he showed delight as he finished off the first and shifted his next step to take down the second wing.

He was having a blast! He was smashing what I built!

I can't say that I handled this first sandcastle building interaction well. Attempt to build. The boy tore it down. Attempt again. He tore it down.

This process went on longer than I would like to admit. I was very frustrated that we couldn't reach an understanding of what was going on.

I don't remember which day it was when I finally gave up the building and just dug a hole.

When I dug a hole, he climbed in and played happily for nearly an hour. Later, he also figured out it was even more fun with water in the bottom. A game emerged where he took a bucket back and forth to the ocean to scoop water for the hole. In most cases, the water soaks immediately back into the sand, though that never discouraged his attempts.

What is my point?

It's one of the most important ideas I should have figured out earlier. I neglected to think enough about the child. I thought about it as my activity.

I had the best of intentions, but I created the activity around my expectations. I built it up in my head around my understanding of what a kid should do on the beach.

I built it up in my mind for me.

One evening on that trip, in the transition from building sandcastles to digging holes, I discussed it with my wife. I complained to her about why the boy wouldn't interact appropriately with the sand.

As she does, she offered me a new perspective.

"He is happy. He is engaged. He is playing on the beach."

The perspective most of us need from time to time, though many of us miss it:

PHILOSOPHIES OF DAILY LIVING

This activity wasn't about me.

This project wasn't about my sandcastle empire.

This time on the beach wasn't about impressing the passerby with my skills in walls and turrets.

The beach activity became the digging of holes.

I've attempted deeper holes.

I've attempted broader holes.

I've attempted holes with higher walls to protect from the oncoming tide.

I admit the walls generally get pulled down just like the castles.

I've attempted a hole for each kid to minimize the fighting. I've dug two holes for the kids with a small connecting canal so they can be part of the same structure. I've even started digging them with open channels in the front so the ocean water can get in there.

Note: though the *"dug to fail"* beach holes get filled in much quicker.

That's ok, though.

You see, the open canal to water, while hastening the demise, increases the temporary enjoyment.

Final Words

I've tried sandcastles again in other years with similar results. They always ended up stepped on or smashed by the shovel very early in the process.

One day in the future, he may need to conform to expectations in this world. But on this day, on this vacation, on this beach:

"H*e is happy. He is engaged, he is playing on the beach.*"

My message here is to build those sandcastles if that's what your family likes. If that isn't their speed, it isn't about you.

Dig some holes.

This moment is all there is

The Money Value of Time

Memoir and parental ephemera at the beach

Are you familiar with the concept of the Time Value of Money?

It's a great concept that can be very important to understand in life.

If you aren't familiar with it, a quick online search gives me a definition that it's the concept where

the money available at present is worth more than the identical sum in the future due to its potential earning capacity.

So a hundred bucks today is worth more than a hundred dollars a few years from now. Yes, that's a pretty basic description, but if you want to look into it further, there are many sources online for more info.

I'm just as interested, if not more interested, in the Money Value of Time.

Can you assign a monetary value to your time?

We've all done that at some time in some way. If we ever worked a job for someone other than ourselves, there's been a certain amount of money that has changed hands for time served or project done.

Even if it's by project not by specific hours, there was a time allotment you gave that project.

If you have a per-hour wage, that may be the most obvious answer for the money value of your time. Minimum wage is a set amount in most places, so someone in a minimum wage job is assigned a specific monetary value for their time.

I've worked multiple jobs with salaries in the past. Although not specified by the hour, there is an expected commitment of time in most positions.

We each make these tradeoffs of our time for money, whether it be in minutes, hours, days, weeks, months, annual, or longer.

Are specific periods worth more than others?

Certain times of day may get higher pay in the hourly wage.

I worked some retail jobs in the past and agreed from time to time to work overnight to restock the store. In these instances, I got an extra dollar an hour for those overnight hours.

Was that not the same eight-hour shift I had worked every other day of the week?

It seems that it was a more valuable period.

Interruption

I know this may not translate later, but at the very moment I'm writing this, my train of thought on this topic has been interrupted as I sit on a shaded picnic table on the deck overlooking the beach.

Interrupted by my seven-year-old (soon to be the middle child) daughter who has decided the clothesline isn't quite enough for the drying of the swimsuits.

She has decided to hang one of them at a time on the end of some random metal pole, no doubt a broken remnant of some excellent beach toy left by a previous renter and wave them in the air like a flag.

That will get them dry quicker!

Now she's hoisted her brother's orange sun shirt and is waving it out over the decking in the sun. Almost lost it to the constant wind but caught it at the last second.

She is giving a running commentary about her plans for when she grows up and wants to start a cleaning business in the rainforest so people can drop their things off for cleaning. Your items would be clean by the end of the day, so you could hang out in the rainforest while your things were cleaned-how convenient!

Now we've moved into stacking shells we've gathered from the beach this week. I started collecting flat sea-worn shell "pebbles" earlier this week and was stacking those. Kids have morphed it into stacking shells and putting as many pebbles in as possible. She has now achieved her "high score" of 18 stacked items.

Now back to the front of the deck with her bright striped pink, yellow, green, orange, blue, white, and then additional pink striped bathing suit foisted on the end of the pole waving in the sun to dry.

These are the tradeoffs that we make.

I work a great job for a salary. Part of the deal is I also get to take paid days off throughout the year. Mine is a deal with a company that is more generous than many.

I guess you could say then that this moment in time, at the picnic table on the shaded deck of a beachfront cottage, has a value.

I still receive my salary for the week because of the arrangements we've made.

But this is also where I struggle with the concept of Money Value of Time because the moment is invaluable.

Invaluable may not be a strong enough word. I hesitate to say one of the most overused words in our culture, but I think this moment may be priceless.

There isn't much that is truly priceless in this world.

There are lots of expensive jewels. There are lots of costly experiences. There are works of art that are hard to value. Some vehicles command high prices at auction. Some treasures are rare and have no equal.

But there is one element that is rarer than all these items.

Time.

We all have access to it, and it is rapidly diminishing and vanishing in front of us every moment of our lives.

This moment is mine. I don't know that there is any dollar amount I would trade for this time. This moment is all there is, and I find it to be priceless.

As she just said, "Keep watching! If you do, something amazing will happen!"

Well, my dear, I'm watching.

Right now.

There are many choices out there

Scales

What are you weighing?

A thought occurred to me recently as I was looking for inspiration

There are many choices out there.

Some options are available to us in different areas based on where we are in our journey. But the options themselves aren't what should drive us-in our decision making framework.

What should drive us is our personal set of scales.

Stay in the metaphorical space with me here, I'm not talking about a physical set of scales, and I'm certainly not talking about that weight scale in the bathroom that some of us feel the need to look back at too often.

I'm talking about the personal judgments we make on what is important to us. I'm talking about the individual thought and consideration we put into decisions that affect our personal, professional, or family lives.

Maybe these scales are tilted for some.

Tilted toward the professional. Maybe some are inclined to the financial. And perhaps some of us have these scales tipped a little toward the personal.

So I guess the real question about these metaphorical scales is

"What are you weighing?"

When you make a choice, do you focus on the options or the overriding goal or outcome you are trying to achieve?

Depending on what you are weighing, if it comes to the point where two options seem to be evenly distributed, where do you put your thumb?

This is an evaluation each of us goes through.

What are you weighing?

And where do you put your thumb?

You choose when to draw the lines

The Ultimate Pie Chart

The pie chart is a fascinating invention.

I'm not sure exactly who first decided to express ideas in the shape of a pie chart though I'm sure it could be traced online. The pie chart is simple. The pie chart is efficient for expressing an idea. It's effective for talking about how much of certain parts make up a whole.

We've all seen them.

The business use is strong. Every presentation needs a pie chart, right?

A circle representing a whole of some sort. A whole of some sort of resource. Any resource you can think of likely has a pie chart somewhere. And we use the pie chart to separate and graphically represent the whole and break it down into another wonderful stat "percentages."

Both can be very good ways to express ideas.

Both can also be very bad way to express ideas.

I didn't really want to talk about business resources in a pie chart today the way one normally thinks about resources in a pie chart.

People in the business world like to get technical on how resources are split in a pie chart and how my pie chart is better than someone else's.

I can build a better pie chart than you can!

I've got better and more vibrant colors on mine!

What I really want to talk about today, now that you are picturing all those advanced pie charts in your head, is the ultimate pie chart.

Think through all those pie charts racing through your head in these business plans or all those business presentations.

What is the ultimate pie chart?

You've seen the ultimate pie chart before.

You've seen the graphical representation of the finite resource that is the most important.

You've already made choices that have determined the percentages.

To make sure we're on the same page here, a percentage is any portion or share in relation to a whole.

You determine the percentage on the ultimate pie chart. Has anyone decoded at this point what their ultimate pie chart is?

---the ultimate pie chart is the Clock---

Picture a round clock face with the seconds. With the minutes.   With the hours. Each time around that clock is twelve hours.

Half a day.

Approximately 7% of a week. We could extrapolate the percentage out to a month, a year, a decade, a lifetime, but I don't want to distract from that round clock face.

That round clock face is the ultimate pie chart.

And you choose the percentages.

You choose where to draw the line and what fills the different categories.

There are other pie charts that matter for specific circumstances and specific choices. Certainly, in a business setting you may review other pie charts for different reasons.

But the real pie chart that you have control over is that pie chart you are moving around in right now.

You decide when to draw the lines in time.

You decide where your percentages are.

You decide who else gets those percentages.

You decide how much those percentages are worth.

The ultimate pie chart is the clock.

Where do you draw the lines?

Create a personal framework

Place Value

Set your feet then set your goals

I always hear words and phrases that have specific meanings in our day to day world and interpret them as something else entirely. I find interest in reimagining names and what they can mean.

A recent example is a math term that came home in my second grader's "Wednesday folder." There was a worksheet telling the parents that they would be working on "place value." My second grader already understood numbers very well, so she didn't have any trouble with the math concept.

But for me? I struggled with this name for a few days. Not the math concept, but the words in that order.

If you're wondering at this point about "place value," the definition I found online is as follows:

Place value: *the numerical value that a digit has by virtue of its position in a number.*

Got it?

In a number, the first number to the left of the decimal

is the one's column. The next number is the ten's column, and the third number is in the hundred's column on into infinity. Thousands, ten thousand, and so forth.

This simple math phrase has been tickling the back of my mind for a couple of days. Now I find the promise of more meaning behind the words.

Place value for me now is something different.

Place value for me is the value represented in our lives by our current place.

Value can be defined differently by each individual and can be determined by your values. For some, this may be a number. A salary number. A bonus number. A street address. The number of hours you get to spend with your family in a given week. This may be a feeling of pride for things you've achieved or what level you've reached in your career.

I believe most of us don't take enough time to think about our own place value. Most of us are too busy thinking about adding value and changing the math with the next promotion, the next raise, or a shiny new car.

"If I could only get to that next level, I'd be happy with my value!"

I'm not saying we shouldn't set goals to change our

current status. We should each have a plan for personal improvement. Think about what you value in your current place and what may or not need to come with you as you plan your next step.

My idea is not to spell out what should be valued. My goal with this brief commentary is to create a personal framework to consider what I value and open the question to others. I believe we should all step back and assess our current situation.

Place value for me is the value represented in our lives by our Current place.

What is your place value?

We've all got something we hold back on

Jam Today

Which quote will you choose?

I've been thinking recently about a former habit in my life where I put off activities until they absolutely had to be done.

In the past, I've considered it procrastination. Sometimes maybe even laziness.

I'm sure I've said "all in good time" every now and then. I also loved that Heinz Ketchup commercial from when I was a kid where the actor was holding the ketchup bottle just waiting for that ketchup to run out.

No hurry.

No rush.

No extra effort needed.

Then the tagline came in "The best things come to those who wait." Even then, at whatever age I was at that point, I thought, "see, I can chill, the best things come to those who wait. No need to get worked up about things." I thought that was a great concept. No hurry.

Don't get so worked up.

"I can't think about that right now. If I do, I'll go crazy. I'll think about that tomorrow.

Some readers may have caught the quote in that last sentence from Scarlett in Gone With the Wind. "I can't think about that right now."

As I've gotten older, though, I've come to view this perspective a little differently. I've found there are different types of activities in life that can be put off and various kinds of activities that can't be put off.

There is nuance in the evaluation of activities that allow a bit of time to plan or put off as the case may be, and there are activities that need more immediate action.

Not only that, our roles change in different periods of our lives.

There is another good exchange between Alice and the White Queen in Lewis Carroll's "Through the Looking Glass." This may seem a little out of context, but the Queen is talking about when jam can be served to Alice if she were to agree to be her lady maid and says.

"The rule is jam tomorrow, and jam yesterday but never jam today."

Then Alice says,

"It must come sometimes to jam today."

To which the Queen replies,

"no, it can't. It's jam every other day. Today isn't any Other day, you know."

This exchange goes back and forth before and after this point in the text, but it really hit me how ridiculous the Queen sounded when I read this recently.

This is a memorable part of where I am now.

I think of some things I've thought about doing.

I wonder about some things I've thought about saying or writing down.

I contemplate some projects I've thought about starting or volunteering for at work.

We've all got something we hold back on. Whatever that is, substitute that in for the word "jam."

Which quote will you choose?

It's a race to see which of these quotes speak to you first.

Do "the best things come to those who wait?

Will you wait for tomorrow?

"After all, tomorrow is another day."

As for me. I'll take it as wisdom from Alice

"it must come sometimes to jam today."

Realize where you are now

Changing Roles
Recognizing where you are now.

In my youth, I had a procrastination problem that I sometimes faced but have had to come to grips with as I've grown up.

I've also noticed that some of the nuance that we see in facing activities we come across has to do with the changing roles we serve in different periods of our lives.

Maybe not just in our lives. I think this change of roles can be applied more broadly to our relationships.

I think our roles change over time in our careers, in our families, maybe in our communities.

A personal story that illustrates this concept happened to me a few years ago.

If you ever meet me in person, I talk about my kids all the time. Having kids has helped me with some crystallization of thought on lots of subjects. But I'm digressing about my personal experience.

Everyone goes through similar changes and phases.

Back to my story.

One day a few years ago when my kids were a little younger than they are at the time of this writing, we were all hanging around the house one evening after school and work.

Well, sometimes I still get surprised. A cute two-year-old unrolls the whole roll of toilet paper into the bowl and clogs the toilet.

Not a great story, right?

Where is this going?

For a few moments I wondered who was going to get the plunger.

My Dad always took care of these sorts of things.

Then it occurred to me.

Oh wait...

"I'm Dad now."

This is what I mean by changing roles. We as human beings have trouble visualizing ourselves in the future. And I think we as human beings also have trouble realizing ourselves in the present.

What has changed for you recently?

Are the important things still the important things?

Has there been a leadership shift at work recently? Maybe you're a new leader?

As we go through different phases of our life, of our career, and in our family, our roles in these areas may change as well.

Maybe you're at a phase where you need more help with specific aspects of life.

Maybe you're at a phase where you are ready to take on more responsibility in your career.

Maybe you have taken on more responsibility in your family.

As a newborn becomes a school kid-a school kid goes off to work-maybe becomes a parent and as the younger become the older there is a nuance in facing activities that we come across with the changing roles we serve in different periods of our lives.

Think about where you've been, yes, but also realize where you are now.

One of the markers for me in recognizing my changing role was my "I'm dad now" moment.

What is your moment?

It's healthy to be a little selfish in life

What is your selfish?
A question for all of us.

Do you think of yourself before others?

How does it feel when I ask?

Are you selfish?

We recoil from the word. I know how it makes me feel.
There is a sense of negativity in selfish.

I want to say an emphatic *"No! I'm not selfish. I'm not all
the negative connotations the world associates with that
word!"*

Let's look at the word itself for a moment and discuss
the meaning.

Defining Selfish (from Dictionary.com)

1. Devoted to or caring only for oneself, concerned
primarily with one's interests, benefits, welfare, etc.
regardless of others.

2. Characterized by or manifesting concern or care only
for oneself.

Is it a bad thing?

Does selfish deserve negativity?

I say "maybe." It can be negative to make choices with no regard for others or with *caring only for oneself.*

I don't think it's fundamentally a bad thing to make choices primarily in one's interests. I think the negativity begins when you add the words *"only for oneself."*

It's healthy to be a little selfish in life.

We may not be in a position to help others until we have our affairs in order.

We plan for our needs. We have our goals as a primary consideration but don't ignore the selfish benefits that helping others can provide. Writing about life experiences can help people, but it also feels good. Giving time to a charitable cause that you find compelling and important can enhance feelings of self-worth.

Based on the definitions above, perhaps it isn't selfish if others are considered. Some things appear and feel selfish that can benefit others if approached properly.

Sometimes it's ok to be a bit selfish if you find a personal selfish that may also help others.

Find your way to do well while also doing good.

What is your selfish?

Outro

I hope you've enjoyed this collection of essays.

I also hope you found the concepts engaging. One thing you find when you do a lot of reading and then a lot of writing personal essays is that patterns emerge. You start to find clarity in your thoughts.

I also noticed that even though they are all personal and could also be considered "memoir" in many cases, emotions are universal.

These are my feelings, but others likely have similar emotions within their own stories.

My philosophies don't have to be your philosophies, but they may make sense to many people. I hope they spur you to think about your own.

I encourage you to circle your favorite in the list. Then take a few moments to write down what it means to you. A word or a sentence is acceptable.

You can find each of these essays on Medium and make a comment or look for me on social media. Put your thoughts out in the world. I'd love to hear your story.

...

MAS

- Write things down
- Acknowledge the truth
- We all need a professor in our lives
- Seek better content
- Make yourself some space
- Everyone has different personalities and preferences
- Time passes differently on vacation
- It isn't about you
- This moment is all there is
- There are many choices our there
- You choose when to draw the lines
- Create a personal framework
- We've all got something we hold back on
- Realize where you are now
- Its healthy to be a little selfish in life